M000160029

# The Cotswold Chef
A YEAR IN RECIPES AND LANDSCAPES

*To Dearest Madge.
All my love,
David

Xmas 2005*

DARIEN-JONES PUBLISHING

*For Ren, Sue & Alex*

# The Cotswold Chef
## A YEAR IN RECIPES AND LANDSCAPES

Rob Rees and Chris Dee
Photography by Nick Darien-Jones

# The Cotswold Chef
## A YEAR IN RECIPES AND LANDSCAPES

Rob Rees and Chris Dee
Photography by Nick Darien-Jones

First published in Great Britain 2005.

ISBN 1-902487-02-8

**Darien-Jones Publishing**
Hillside House, Pitchcombe,
Gloucestershire GL6 6LN,
United Kingdom.

**www.thecotswoldchef.com**

# Contents

Cover photo: Stroud – famous for its Five Valleys.
Title page photo: The Painswick Valley from Pitchcombe in Autumn.
Left: Bisley in May.

# How to Use this Book

This book is a guide to, and celebration of, the Cotswold year in food.

In these pages we suggest some seasonal recipes, include a monthly guide to what's fresh when and give away a few secrets on how to get the most from your food shopping at Farmers' Markets and elsewhere. The message is 'buy local', match your cooking to the seasons and have fun.

Each Cotswold season is introduced in turn, with photographs by Nick Darien-Jones and Rob Rees' recipe ideas. For those who like to copy recipes exactly, these give exciting ways to use what's seasonally available – for the rest of us they provide further inspiration on what to look for in the markets.

*Mid-Summer sunrise in the Uley Valley.*

The aim of this book is to encourage you to share in the Cotswold lifestyle – which means a more relaxed pace of life, a direct relationship with the people who produce your food and enjoyment of time, conversation and food with friends and family. Reflecting this spirit, the recipes in this book are usually for four or six people.

For the reader outside the Cotswolds, pages 20 and 21 offer advice on finding alternatives to the local ingredients quoted.

7

# Rob Rees - The Cotswold Chef

Rob Rees is a chef who has lived and worked in the Cotswolds for over 10 years.

The Cotswold hills are an agricultural area with a culinary inheritance that includes Double Gloucester cheese, Old Spot pork and well-kept secrets that locals tend to be rather proud of, such as Blaisdon Red plums and River Severn elvers. These ingredients are slowly being rediscovered by a wider audience, and yet Rob would be the first to avoid nostalgia for the sake of it. A new generation of food producers is, for example, now growing chilli peppers, artichokes and other non traditional crops.

After a warm family upbringing where food played an important part, Rob Rees' early experience was gained at the Royal Crescent Hotel in Bath, the Hyatt Regency in the Grand Cayman Islands, Le Gavroche in London and the Bath Spa Hotel. Rob has been Head Chef at Circus in Bath and Splinters in Christchurch.

Between 1994 and 1999 Rob was chef-proprietor of the Country Elephant in Painswick, a highly successful restaurant that achieved a much-coveted Michelin Bibendum Gourmand Award.

It feels now as if Farmers' Markets have been around for ever, but it was in 1999 that the Cotswold food scene changed dramatically, with the celebrated Stroud Farmers' Market starting in July of that year. Rob Rees was involved from early on, running seasonal food demonstrations at the

*Above left and right: Rob Rees buying local produce.*
*Left: The former Country Elephant Restaurant in Painswick.*

8

market and building up a local following that soon extended to BBC radio and local press – and then to BBC Good Food Live. After a chance meeting with the local tourist board, Rob has found himself in places as far away as India and Hong Kong representing the combined appeal of Britain's food and tourism attractions. Rob has enjoyed such challenges as introducing French food writers to English cheeses, the Japanese to Cotswold trout and Australians to local lamb.

The Farmers' Market movement has been an important phenomenon in the Cotswolds and has re-awoken positive curiosity about food – what to buy and when, how to prepare local raw materials and how food contributes to family life and the joy of living in this beautiful area – all themes close to Rob's heart. Hand-in-hand with the development of Farmers' Markets has been the

improvement in farm shops and their contribution to the struggle to provide a realistic alternative to supermarkets.

Rob Rees has become a recognised communicator about food, nutrition and the pleasures of cooking and sharing food in the home. He continues to live and work in the Cotswolds and enjoys demonstrating the quality of food derived from the Cotswold landscape. The times have finally caught up with him and his passion for communicating the 'real food' message is in demand. At Rob's home, near the pretty Cotswold village of Bisley, a purpose built demonstration kitchen is opening up new possibilities for cookery lessons and events with The Cotswold Chef.

*Above: Christmas Pudding cookery lesson.*
*Above right: Allotments at Far Oakridge.*
*Right: Sycamore tree in Miserden.*

The beautiful working environment of the Cotswolds produces some of the best food on earth. We hope that this book will help you and your family to experiment, enjoy the seasonality of real food and to have the confidence to know what to look for in the markets, whatever the time of year.

9

## The Cotswold Year - A Food Buyer's Guide

### JANUARY

Allotment holders say that a bit of frost never does root vegetables any harm and this is a great month for strong earthy flavours. Keep thinking about warming soups and pot roasts and life can be great – even in the bleakest January! It's a good month for game too, with partridge coming into their peak of maturity, pheasant everywhere on pub menus, and mallard, pigeon, rabbit and hare offered by serious butchers. Venison is good at this time of year too.

This month usually sees the last of English apples and pears at their best.

### FEBRUARY

Brussels sprouts, salsify and shallots are around this month. If the weather is mild, you can tell yourself that Spring is here by looking out for wild chives, forced lettuce, very early spring onions and chicory.

Most wild or farmed venison is also now at its rich, dark and succulent prime – the flavour is absolutely superb. Remember that wild venison will require some kind of marinade and benefits from slower cooking, like a casserole. Juniper and venison is a classic combination.

Valentine's Day in February has now turned into something of a week-long celebration with cards and chocolates and every restaurant booked in advance. It may sound odd coming from a former restaurateur, but February 14th is one night of the year that I always plan to stay in to prepare a romantic dinner at home. What could be more romantic than cooking at home together?

*Painswick from Edge in January.*

# MARCH

Calabrese, purple sprouting, broccoli, carrots, spring greens and spring onion make their appearance in March, as does early rhubarb.

Spring lamb appears, but is not at its peak yet. Wild garlic starts to take hold in the woods and moist valleys around our home in the south Cotswolds. Spring flowers colour the garden and there's a sense that everything is getting interesting for the chef again.

With the feeling that hearty Winter cooking is over, it's a good month to visit one of the Cotswold trout farms or the Severn and Wye Smokery and bring home a little added freshness and variety.

*Broadway from West End, late March.*

11

## APRIL & MAY

These Spring months are a delight in the Cotswolds. At weekends, popular towns and villages such as Broadway, Stow-on-the-Wold, Burford and Tetbury become busy, but there are hundreds of quieter villages to escape to. For me, a larger

Cotswold village isn't complete without a pub and I always look out for a simple short menu with local ingredients. It's always a positive sign when a pub lists suppliers on the blackboard or menu and when staff are obviously knowledgeable about the produce on offer. And the more people who ask about suppliers, the more likely pubs and restaurants are to take local food sourcing seriously.

In the markets, look out for cabbages and carrots, leeks, new potatoes (starting with Jersey and Cornwall produce) and possibly some early lettuce. You'll also see early broad beans, spinach, sorrel and primo cabbage.

In May, asparagus from nearby Evesham is probably the best in the world and the best pubs serve it simply with butter, new potatoes and home-baked ham.

## JUNE

With Summer on the way, courgettes, globe artichokes, green beans, salad leaves and mange-tout are in the markets. Cotswold strawberries are readily available and delicious and there's a great opportunity to protest against bland supermarket fruit varieties by getting out to the nearest 'pick your own' farm.

Little Gems and Romaine lettuces lift any salad. They have crispness and intensity – perfect for Caesar salad with garlic, anchovy and grated Parmesan, or maybe just split, washed and topped with poached eggs, crispy Old Spot bacon and some apple and raisin dressing.

*Top left: A Cotswold farmer sorts lambs from ewes, near Tunley Bottom.*
*Left: Chalford's Golden Valley.*
*Right: The lower ford at Kineton.*

13

## JULY

Things get very 'English' in July with broad beans, peas and runner beans, cucumbers, lettuces and leaves, radishes and watercress.

With a little imagination and some great local produce this is the time for light Summer dishes. Peas loosened from the pod explode sweetness. Tender young broad beans are sublime in salads or velvety soups. Try gently parboiling and then sauté with a touch of crushed fresh garlic, grated ginger and a splash of cream. Dice some local fresh cheese like a Ruddle Court Camembert with chopped mint and a mix of beans, a drizzle of oil and a little lime zest and you have a fantastic lunch dish.

Enjoy fresh and healthy black, red and white currants, gooseberries, strawberries and raspberries.

## AUGUST

August is a herby time. Basil fills ou with a strong flavour that needs to be treated with respect. Coriander is growing well too. If you love salads and find yourself buying supermarket bags, then shame on you, especially at this time of year when Farmers' Markets and farm shops provide better value and freshness. Wild food lovers should hunt out nasturtium flowers – which give a lovely, peppery lift to salads

You'll also see new beetroots, courgettes, peppers, sweetcorn and plenty of varieties of tomatoes around. The globe artichoke is at it best now, with a bulb rich in flavou and very nutritious.

*Left: 'Gloucester' cattle – the source of Singl and Double Gloucester cheeses – graze in an apple orchard at Wick Court Farm. Right: Lower Slaughter Mill.*

14

# SEPTEMBER

September is heaven for fruit and pudding lovers. Plums, greengages and blackberries appear and wild sloes and elderberries are seen on the hedgerows.

Salads continue well into September, followed by the beginning of the wild mushroom season.

Chards are back on the menu in September in almost every rainbow colour. Ruby Chard offers sweetness

in its stems and leaves that can be a delightful accompaniment to a lightly grilled trout fillet – season it as you sauté with a little nutmeg.

I've never been a huge fan of beetroot, but it's often passed over the garden wall by a neighbour in September and a little home experimentation has converted me. I had been put off by its earthiness, but try coating lightly with a fine balsamic vinegar and a pinch of sugar after its first steam or boil. *Delicious!*

Red onions also start to be pulled in abundance during September – one of my real favourites and very versatile. Roast them on a barbecue or confit slowly with oregano and red wine for one of my family favourites.

# OCTOBER

The beech tree is the star of Cotswold woodland. In October it colours the Cotswolds and, at around the same time, an explosion of colour hits the farm shops and markets.

Broccoli, cabbage, marrows and squashes join potatoes and young turnips to make this an exciting month for the cook. At home, a kind of nesting instinct takes over and I find myself stocking up on logs for the fire, sweeping away the golden leaves scattered on the lawn and perhaps bottling apple, plum and greengage chutneys. I also start to think about Christmas cake and Christmas Puddings.

Autumn is also the season for wild mushrooms – look out for ceps, chanterelles, horse and field mushrooms. It's also worth investigating fresh walnuts and chestnuts. Apples and pears are excellent at this time.

## NOVEMBER

For me, November is all about cosiness and cuddles, crisp frosty morning walks and warming, hearty lunches and suppers. In fact, the food around at this time of year encourages this feeling with parsnips, turnips, beetroots, Savoy cabbages, carrots, cauliflowers, celeriac, celery and leeks in the markets. Game such as pheasant and partridge is just coming into its own.

Tradition has it that the household pig was slaughtered during November – this would be made into bacon and ham to keep the family fed through the Winter. These days, pork is exceptional the whole year and the Gloucester Old Spot breed is enjoying popularity again. Other breeds are equally good in flavour – talk to your butcher or producer at the market for enlightenment and cooking ideas. I love a slow roasted loin of pork on Winter vegetables.

# DECEMBER

Pear season also really takes a hold during November – do remember that pears won't improve much with time if you pick them, unlike many other fruits. Store them at room temperature until you are ready to use them in dishes such as pear tatins, soufflés or mousses.

Curly kale, Jerusalem artichokes, leeks, garlic, pumpkin, swedes, chard and spinach are all available to provide variety and freshness before and during Christmas.

Chestnuts and sprouts deserve more attention at this time of year.

Fresh chestnuts are well worth finding. Not only will they encourage you to burst into song re: open fires and roasting, but the taste is fantastic. Cut little slits in the outer skin (so that they don't explode during baking) then roast them gently. While they're still warm, peel back the skin and enjoy... or take them to a pan with a little touch of garlic butter, rosemary and Cajun spice.

Brussels sprouts amaze me! So much flavour comes out of such a tiny ball of green. Trim off the outer leaves, place a small cross in the stem and boil gently for five minutes.
I love to fry them off with some pancetta, cumin and pine nuts.

*Far left: Wick Street.*
*Left: Low Winter sun.*

17

# Getting the Most from Farm Shops and Markets

The best local food will reward you with flavours you've forgotten about.

Farm shops and markets can put the fun back into food shopping. Instead of studying labels and serving suggestions from supermarket boxes, it's really rewarding to go to markets and meet producers. Don't forget to ask them how they use their own produce – often you'll get the best cooking advice that way.

Here are some things to keep in mind when you visit a market or shop – or a supermarket, for that matter.

## Get there early

Obviously, the best sells first. Some foods have a limited season – for example apple juice, from the best suppliers, can get scarce in the Summer. The best cheeses 'sell-out' too.

## Just because it's local... it doesn't always mean it's great

It's tempting to assume that because produce is 'local' it must be better – but it's not necessarily so. In fact there will always be good, average and poor producers.

In many cases, you can try before you buy, but sometimes you'll just have to go back to the basics of market buying. Look for queues – certain stalls are always busy for a good reason. Talk to producers – if they're proud and enthusiastic about what they're selling, you'll probably enjoy it too. And check exactly how local the food on offer really is. The best Farmers' Markets enforce a 'miles travelled' limit on suppliers.

Look for award certificates and ask why they were won. A food hygiene certificate should be on display.

## Is organic best?

It's also tempting to assume that organics are best, but I don't follow this as a rigid rule. It's more important that food is well produced. One of my favourite apple juices, for example, isn't organic – but it might as well be.

To me, organics have a role to play but not to the extent of excluding non-organic foods. Other issues, such as free range or price are as important.

Don't forget that organics such as bread or sausages may have a shorter shelf life without all those preservatives. Plan and buy accordingly.

18

*Shopping at Stroud Farmers' Market.*

## Experiment

Most chefs would encourage you to tear up the shopping list and just buy what looks good.

One approach I always encourage is to put more emphasis on vegetables. For example, a great piece of lamb, simply roasted, will have flavours that shine through without the need to do anything too clever. However, serve with some shallots baked as a vegetable with a touch of white wine, cinnamon, honey and cracked pepper and the combination will wow your guests.

Rejoice in the fact that you will encounter new and unfamiliar tastes and smells at a Farmers' Market – remember that the alternative is blandness, over packaging and wasted money! A day out food shopping with children will teach you all something new, especially as

children have a fascination with food and the innocence to stop, look and ask interesting questions.

At a time when supermarket customers can buy African mange-tout in December, shopping at farm shops and Farmers' Markets should give you a head start on the seasonality front, but there are 'right' times of year to buy fruit, vegetables, meat and even cheeses, so a little research is always repaid.

## Country Markets

With the best will in the world, I don't always feel like making food from scratch. I quite often find myself buying pickles, jams and cakes from Country Markets and I'm rarely disappointed – the love and respect for ingredients that I try to put into my own cooking is usually there as well!

## Quality not quantity

It's been proved that food is often cheaper at markets and farm shops, but be prepared to pay a premium for quality sometimes. An artisan-made local cheese will make a much bigger after-dinner impact than an entire boxed cheese 'selection'. If you're watching the cost, remember to compare like with like.

19

## Cotswold specialities and alternatives

The recipes in this book often refer to local Cotswold varieties and produce. For alternatives, here is some chef's advice on what to look for.

### Beef

Beef should be moist and firm with a dark red colour, flecks of fat and no blood. The white fat produces an effect called marbling and this should be dry, creamy white in colour and odourless. Vacuum-packed meat tends to regain this red colour a few minutes after opening. It's thought that vacuum packing reduces the vitamins in meat and so ask your favourite producer if they sell through a butchers without packing.

The Gloucester breed of cow (photo on page 14) makes for especially creamy milk, cream and cheese. Every year in May, a Gloucester cheese is chased down the steep slope at Cooper's Hill in the Cotswolds in a tradition that links local food and the landscape nicely!

### Pork

Gloucester Old Spot (photo above) is a fatty, flavoursome variety distinguished by a spot on its back and the legend that this is caused by apples falling onto the animal in Gloucestershire orchards.

When buying pork, look for rose pink flesh with a good distribution of fat. The fat is full of flavour and will spread throughout the joint as it cooks, especially if you remember to baste regularly. Don't buy meat that is discoloured, slightly dewy in appearance or (obviously) smelly.

### Lamb

The meat should be a dull red with a fine grain. The fat in lamb should be evenly distributed with a flaky texture and a clear white colour. For better value, look at chops, shoulders and shanks of lamb instead of saddles, legs and racks.

### Game and Poultry

Game provides some of the most honest flavours in Cotswold cooking. It is seasonal and it pays to get to know a supplier that you can trust – to avoid being offered the previous season's frozen pheasant for example. You can roast whole birds or pan fry perfectly well up to about Christmas – after that things get a bit tough and braising will be better.

Guinea Fowl are a great bargain – cook them just like chicken. Duck legs are also excellent value.

20

If you are buying chicken, look for dry skin and remember that free range legs of chicken can be a good value, flavourful alternative to chicken breasts. Quality chickens sold at farm shops and markets tend to be of mixed sizes – adapt your recipe accordingly.

## Vegetables

**Broccoli** should be firm and dark green in colour. It's available year round from supermarkets but, as with so many ingredients, British broccoli is far superior in the right season.

**Brussels sprouts** are best when small, dark green and not opened up too much. They always improve after they have experienced a good frost (it breaks down the starch and turns it into sugar) and so consider advance preparation and freezing before use.

Young **carrots** should just be scrubbed clean and the skins left intact – this is where all the vitamin C is. Older or large carrots should be peeled and sliced. It's said that they keep an earthy taste if sliced across and a sweet one if sliced lengthways – worth a try!

Strong leaves and a creamy white colour are signs of a good **cauliflower**. When buying **leeks** – look for dark green leaves and a firm stem. **Parsnips** should be firm, creamy white and free from too many brown marks.

**Peas** convert their natural sweetness into starch as soon as they are harvested and so shouldn't be stored – ask when they were picked.

**Potatoes** come in many named varieties. If in doubt, the basic distinction is between floury types (such as King Edward) or waxy types (such as Cara). Floury potatoes have a dry texture when cooked and make the best mashed, boiled or chipped potatoes. Waxy potatoes don't make for good mash, but are great for baked and layered recipes. If you don't know what you've bought, put one into some very salty water – a waxy potato will float. Varieties like Wilja or Estima are all-rounders.

When buying potatoes check that they are firm. Look out for green skin (caused by exposure to light) and avoid. Green patches are also a tell tale sign on **swedes**, although their skins naturally range from cream through to purple. Avoid cracked skins.

21

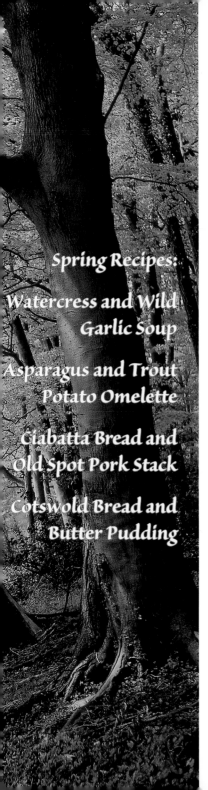

Spring Recipes:

Watercress and Wild
Garlic Soup

Asparagus and Trout
Potato Omelette

Ciabatta Bread and
Old Spot Pork Stack

Cotswold Bread and
Butter Pudding

# Spring - Wild Flowers and Wild Garlic

Anyone who has experienced a really cold Cotswold Winter will immediately understand the pleasure that comes with the arrival of Spring. Snowdrops are followed by daffodils and bluebells and there's a sensual pleasure in watching nature come to life again.

For the cook, wild garlic is the first free crop of the year. It's a seasonal treat that I use here in a watercress and wild garlic soup. Even unpicked, they are a delight, with a powerful scent in the lanes around home and, later, precise small white flower heads carpeting the woodland.

Spring is the season of lambs in the field and constant signs of rebirth. Actually, Cotswold lamb is at its best in early summer, but joys such as asparagus, rhubarb and our local Gloucester Old Spot pork find their way into the kitchen in this season.

*Bluebells in beech woods, April.*

*Distinctive Cotswold beech woods, with fresh new leaves in Spring.*

23

## Watercress and Wild Garlic Soup

Serves 6

2 bunches of washed and shredded "Purely Organics" watercress

1lb (450g) "Duchy Home Farm" leeks, washed and finely chopped

1 washed, peeled and chopped medium potato

2oz (50g) "Netherend Farm" butter

6floz (175ml) "Cotteswold Dairy" double cream

$1\frac{1}{2}$pt (850ml) vegetable stock

Black pepper

5 leaves of wild garlic, washed and finely sliced

3floz (75ml) "Day's Cottage" apple juice

1. Melt the **butter** in a thick-bottomed saucepan. Add the **leeks**, **potatoes** and **watercress**.

2. Pour in the **apple juice** and then cover with a lid and allow to simmer for 15 minutes. Take care to stir from time to time, to avoid burning.

3. Add the **stock**. Bring to simmering point again for another 10 minutes or until the vegetables are all tender.

4. Remove from the heat and allow to cool.

5. Place in a liquidiser and puree until smooth.

6. Return to saucepan to reheat and serve with a twist of **pepper** and the **double cream**.

7. At the moment of serving add the **wild garlic**. Its pungent smell and flavour will be released instantly.

24

## Asparagus and Trout Potato Omelette

Serves 4

4 "Cotswold Legbar" eggs

$\frac{1}{2}$oz (12g) farm butter

Drizzle of "Selsley Herb" olive oil

2 medium "Duncan Paget" potatoes, washed, peeled and diced into 5mm cubes

2 finely chopped rashers of "Scrubditch Farm" bacon (optional for veggies)

1 chopped "Abbey Farm" red onion

3oz (75g) crumbled "Ruddle Court" cheese

Black pepper

4oz (110g) washed, trimmed and blanched "Evesham" asparagus spears (use the trimmings for soup)

2 fillets of "Cockleford" trout

*Above left: Wild garlic in flower.*
*Left: Cotswold barns, Duntisbourne Leer.*
*Right: Temple Guiting Church.*

1. *Melt the **butter** and **oil** together in a frying pan.*

2. *Fry the diced **potato** till lightly golden (about 6 minutes).*

3. *Next add the **bacon**, **trout**, **onions** and cook till soft. These will need a twist of **pepper** from the mill.*

4. *Add the **asparagus spears** and half of the **cheese**.*

5. *Beat the **eggs** with a fork and pour into frying pan. Cook on a high heat.*

6. *Loosen from around the edges so that any raw egg can escape around the outer edge.*

7. *Sprinkle the rest of the **cheese** over the top and place under a very hot grill for a few minutes until the egg is thoroughly cooked and the topping is crisp and golden brown.*

8. *Serve either whole or in wedges with a mixture of some roughly cut washed **garden herbs** and an extra drizzle of oil.*

25

## Ciabatta Bread and Old Spot Pork Stack

Serves 4

8oz (225g) hummus

1 punnet mustard cress

1 red pepper

1 green pepper

1 yellow pepper

1 punnet "Over Farm" baby tomatoes on the vine

2 sprigs of "Selsley Herb" rosemary

2 sprigs lemon thyme

"Hobbs House" ciabatta bread

2 tbsps olive oil

1oz (25g) of "Netherend Farm" butter

1 lime

2 x 8oz (225g) "Scrubditch Meats" Old Spot pork loin steaks

1 chopped clove of garlic

1 tsp cracked black pepper

1. De-seed and cut the **peppers** into 4.

2. Heat a pan with a little **olive oil** and chopped **garlic**.

3. Add the **peppers** and gently fry. Season them.

4. Warm the **bread** in the oven on a low heat.

5. Slice and spread the **hummus** evenly over the pieces of **bread** once warmed.

6. Heat a pan with **olive oil** and **garlic**. Once hot add the **butter** and melt till golden brown. Add the **pork steak** – presentation side first into the pan. Cook till golden then turn and repeat on other side. Test that the juices in the meat are running clear before serving.

7. Season with cracked **black pepper** and the zest and juice of **lime**.

8. Serve cut into slices as a stack with the **bread**, **peppers** and **mustard cress**.

9. Accompany with lightly grilled tomatoes on the vine and some "Selsley Herb" chutney.

26

# Cotswold Bread and Butter Pudding

## Serves 6

1pt (575ml) "Cotteswold Dairy" milk

3oz (75g) sugar

2 "Cotswold Legbar" eggs

3 "Cotswold Legbar" egg yolks

1 split vanilla pod

Grated nutmeg

Zest of orange

6oz (175g) raisins

8 slices of "Hobbs House" fruit bread or plain white bread

3oz (75g) "Netherend Farm" butter

Dash of vanilla vodka!

*1. Soak the **raisins** in the **vodka** for an hour. Meanwhile heat the oven to 180°C (gas mark 4).*

*2. Butter the sliced **fruit bread** and remove the crusts. Cut into triangles.*

*3. Whisk the **eggs** and **sugar** together in a suitable sized bowl.*

*4. Place the **vanilla pod**, **nutmeg** and grated **orange zest** into the pan with the **milk**.*

*5. Bring the **milk** to simmer.*

*6. Pour onto the **egg mix** and whisk.*

*7. Sprinkle the bottom of a baking dish with the **raisins**.*

*8. Neatly arrange the **buttered bread**.*

*9. Strain the **milk** mix over the top and bake in a moderate oven in a 'Bain Marie' (water bath) for approximately 45 minutes.*

*10. Once golden and firm remove from the oven, sprinkle with **caster sugar** and serve.*

*Above left: Cotswold dwelling at Barton.*
*Left: Spring landscape near Far Oakridge.*
*Right: Owlpen Church and Manor.*

27

**Summer Recipes:**

**Risotto of English Peas, Stinging Nettles, Broad Beans, Mint and Blue Cheese**

**...ard, Herb and Celeriac ...ash' with Horseradish Spiced Lamb**

**Strawberries in English Tarragon and Lavender Custard**

**Marinated Summer Berries with Cotswold Meringues**

# Summer - Beans and Berries

I make no excuse for including two Summer season pudding recipes. Our strawberries are surely the best in the world and I like to combine them with a lavender custard for a fully English experience.

Summer is also a great opportunity to ensure that the most is made of seasonal peas and beans – always make sure that they have been recently picked (or pick your own) to ensure that they are delicious rather than starchy.

Simplicity is the true virtue of Summer. Flavours often naturally fall into place with a minimal need for cooking, giving every opportunity to indulge in the garden with a chilled glass of wine, perhaps a pitcher of Pimm's and some great conversation with friends.

*Cotswold escarpment at dawn.*

*Snowshill Lavender Farm in July.*

29

## Risotto of English Peas, Stinging Nettles, Broad Beans, Mint and Blue Cheese

Serves 4 - 6

8oz (225g) arborio risotto rice

6oz (175g) peas and 6oz (175g) broad beans from the Farmers' Market – both freshly podded

2oz (50g) chopped garden mint

1 finely chopped onion

4oz (110g) diced "Birdwood Farm" blue cheese

2fl oz (50ml) "Day's Cottage" apple juice

6fl oz (175ml) "Luscombe" ginger ale

$1/4$pt (150ml) vegetable stock

1oz (25g) "Netherend Farm" butter

Drizzle of "Selsley Herb" olive oil

1oz (25g) grated or sushi ginger

12 washed stinging nettle leaves, sautéed in butter (treat like spinach)

Zest of 1 lime

1. *Sweat the* **onion** *in a mixture of a little* **olive oil** *and* **butter***.*

2. *Add the* **rice** *and stir into the* **onions** *so that the grains of rice are completely coated with the oil.*

3. *Mix all of the* **liquid ingredients** *together in one container.*

4. *Add the liquid to the rice little by little – ideally in three batches.*

5. *After each addition, take care to gently simmer the liquid away. Stir the rice all the time.*

6. *Once all the liquid is absorbed, check the texture of the rice. If it is soft with just a little bite then it is ready. If still too hard, add some water.*

7. *Just prior to serving, add the* **vegetables***,* **nettles** *and the* **blue cheese***.*

8. *Mix together gently over the heat. The cheese will just melt slightly to bind the risotto together.*

9. *Take care not to overcook at this stage, as the fresh, vibrant colours of the vegetables are essential. Finally add the* **ginger***,* **lime zest** *and* **mint***.*

*Serve with some fresh watercress and perhaps some smoked fish.*

*Don't forget that those with allergies should use caution when preparing and eating nettles.*

*The water-mill at Donnington Brewery.*

30

## Chard, Herb and Celeriac 'Hash' with Horseradish Spiced Lamb

Serves 4

3 parboiled "Duchy Home Farm" potatoes, thinly sliced

3 large "Washbrook Farm" chard leaves

1 small celeriac, peeled, washed and diced small

1 chopped clove of garlic

½ chopped "Duncan Paget" onion

1 tsp caraway seeds

1 tsp turmeric

Freshly chopped thyme

12oz (325g) lean "Whitfield Farm" lamb meat cut into strips

1 tsp "Kitchen Garden Foods" horseradish relish or grated fresh horseradish

1 chopped "Duchy Home Farm" red chilli

1 tsp clear "Four Shires" honey

1 tsp cracked black pepper

Fresh "Purely Organics" watercress

1 tsp of "Selsley Herb" wholegrain mustard

Olive oil

*For the Hash:*

*1. In a non-stick pan, gently fry the onion, garlic, and caraway seeds with a drizzle of olive oil, until soft.*

*2. Add half of the roughly chopped chard. Cook for a further minute to allow it to soften.*

*3. Add the potatoes and celeriac and season with thyme and turmeric. Mix together gently.*

*4. Sauté gently on medium heat.*

*For the Lamb:*

*1. Heat a pan with olive oil.*

*2. Add the chopped garlic and chilli and cook for a few moments to let the flavours out.*

*3. Add the lamb strips and cook in a similar way to a stir fry (quickly on a high heat to seal the outside of the lamb).*

*4. Add the mustard, horseradish, pepper, honey and remaining chard.*

*5. Place the hash onto a large platter and place the horseradish lamb into the centre with some watercress leaves and a generous drizzle of olive oil and cracked black pepper.*

*This is a great dish just to get stuck into as a group of friends, with some crunchy bread and summer salads.*

31

## Strawberries in English Tarragon and Lavender Custard

Serves 2 – with seconds!

1 punnet of strawberries or mixed summer berries "A & A Fruit Farm"

A few hand picked wild strawberries

3 "Cotswold Legbar" egg yolks

2 "Cotswold Legbar" eggs

2oz (50g) caster sugar

1 tsp of "Lypiatt House" honey

Chopped "Selsley Herb" tarragon

1 cinnamon stick

1 split vanilla pod

2 "Cotswold Meringue Company" meringues

$\frac{1}{2}$pt (275ml) of "Cotteswold Dairy" fresh cream

2 scoops of "Winstone's" ice cream or yoghurt

Just over 1oz (25g) of picked "Snowshill Farm" lavender flower

1. Wash and hull the **strawberries** and place in a bowl.

2. Whisk together the **eggs**, **yolks**, **sugar** and **honey**.

3. Bring the **cream**, **vanilla**, **cinnamon**, **tarragon** and half the **lavender** to the boil.

4. Once boiled, pour onto the **egg mixture**, stir well and return to the heat.

5. On a slow heat, whisk or stir continuously until the mix thickens. This is the egg cooking. To test it is ready, see if the mixture coats the back of a spoon. (Take care not to over-cook or you will have scrambled egg!)

6. Pour over the **strawberries** and allow to infuse.

7. Serve by placing a **meringue** in the centre of a bowl and fill with some of the **custard mix**.

8. Place a scoop of **ice cream** in the centre and top with a further amount of berries.

9. Perhaps drizzle with a local **honey**. Try some fresh **mint**, a sprinkling of the remaining **lavender**, dusting of icing sugar and a few **wild strawberries** to serve.

32

## Marinated Summer Berries with Cotswold Meringues

### Serves 4

**4 "Cotswold Meringue Company" meringue nests**

**1 large punnet of "Over Farm" strawberries, washed, hulled and quartered**

**1 punnet of washed "Over Farm" raspberries**

**A handful of washed blackcurrants and redcurrants**

**Juice of 2 lemons**

**1oz (25g) icing sugar**

**1 tsp of crushed black peppercorns**

**2 finely chopped "Selsley Herb" basil leaves**

**"Winstone's" ice cream**

*Left: Late Summer harvested field.*
*Right: The Cotswolds sees many village fêtes during the Summer months – great places to buy plants, herbs and strawberries.*

1. *Simply place all the **berries** in a bowl.*

2. *Add all of the other ingredients and mix together well.*

3. *Do this gently so as not to mash the berries.*

4. *Allow to soak for 2 hours and then serve on top of the **meringue nests**.*

5. *You may want to add a scoop of your favourite fruit sorbet or **ice cream**.*

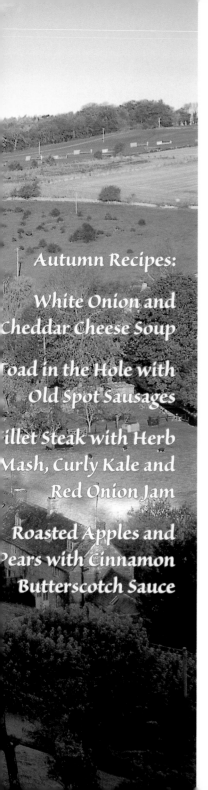

Autumn Recipes:

White Onion and Cheddar Cheese Soup

Toad in the Hole with Old Spot Sausages

Fillet Steak with Herb Mash, Curly Kale and Red Onion Jam

Roasted Apples and Pears with Cinnamon Butterscotch Sauce

# Autumn Colours

Autumn is surely the best time to be in the Cotswolds. The beech trees blaze a trail of colour across the landscape, the air has a refreshing cool bite and it's the time to enjoy walks before Winter sets in.

Autumn is also an exciting time for a cook to be at work in the Cotswolds. Head to your local Farmers' Market and rediscover the great taste of vegetables grown locally and harvested recently. Seasonal vegetables include curly kale, carrots, parsnips, turnips, fennel, spinach, celeriac, garlic, leeks and onions.

When cooking one or more from the above list, I like to prepare them in the normal way, drain off liquid carefully and then add a touch of butter, a drizzle of honey and some finely chopped rosemary. Sauté for an extra minute and serve.

*Autumn sun chases away frost at Naunton.*

*Sheepwash, near Lower Swell.*

35

## White Onion and Cheddar Cheese Soup

Serves 6

1¹/₂lb (700g) sliced "Abbey Farm" white onions

1oz (25g) butter

6oz (175g) "Godsell's Church Farm" cheddar cheese

2 medium potatoes, washed, peeled and cubed

1 sprig of thyme

1 bay leaf

1pt (575ml) vegetable stock

Black pepper

Pinch of nutmeg

3fl oz (75ml) "Cotteswold Dairy" whipping cream

1. Melt the **butter** in a thick-bottomed pan.

2. Add the **onions**, **thyme**, **nutmeg** and **potato** and gently sweat together for approximately 3 minutes.

3. Cover with the **stock** and bring to the boil.

4. Allow to simmer for 15 minutes or until the potato is tender.

5. Remove from the heat and allow to cool slightly.

6. Liquidise until smooth and then strain through a sieve into a clean saucepan.

7. When you are ready to serve, reheat and add the **cheese** in three equal measures. Ensure that you whisk each handful into the soup thoroughly. Add the **pepper** and the **whipping cream** and serve.

## Toad in the Hole with Old Spot Sausages

Serves 4

8oz (225g) "Shipton Mill" plain flour

6 "Jaxons Farm" eggs

¹/₂pt (275ml) milk

1 tsp of "Kitchen Garden Foods" mustard

6 Gloucestershire Old Spot or equivalent pork sausages

1 finely chopped "Duchy Home Farm" onion

1oz (25g) "Netherend Farm" butter

For the Batter:

1. Beat the **eggs**, **milk** and **mustard** together with a whisk.

2. Place **flour** in a bowl and make a well in the centre.

3. Add the liquid and gradually mix in the flour to make a 'dropping consistency' batter. Allow to rest for 1 hour before baking.

36

*For the Toad:*

*1. Melt the **butter** in a frying pan. Just when the butter turns golden brown, add the **sausages**.*

*2. Allow the sausages to become golden brown all over, but not fully cooked. Next add the chopped **onion** and fry for a further minute.*

*3. Place the **sausages** and **onions** mix in a deep ovenproof dish.*

*4. Pour the **batter** over the sausages so that they are (just over) half covered. Place in a hot oven to bake for 30 minutes.*

*5. The batter will rise like a Yorkshire pudding, going extremely crisp on the top. The juices in the sausages should run clear.*

*6. Serve piping hot from the oven.*

*Autumn trees, Ullenwood.*

## Fillet Steak with Herb Mash, Curly Kale and Red Onion Jam

Serves 2

2 x 8oz (225g) "Adey's Farm" fillet steaks

1 large finely sliced red onion

1 red chilli

1 sprig of "Selsley Herb" thyme

1 chopped clove of garlic

2oz (50g) caster sugar or local honey

1 glass red wine or Port

8oz (225g) curly kale or spinach

$4\frac{1}{2}$fl oz (125ml) fresh "Day's Cottage" apple juice

1 tsp nutmeg

1 large "Duncan Paget" baking potato

Chopped fresh parsley

Chopped fresh coriander

$4\frac{1}{2}$fl oz (125ml) olive oil

1fl oz (25ml) balsamic vinegar

$4\frac{1}{2}$oz (125g) grated "Godsell's Church Farm" strong cheddar

Cracked black pepper

1 bunch "Purely Organics" watercress

3oz (75g) "Netherend Farm" butter

*For the Mash:*

*1. Place the **potato** in a saucepan and cover with water. Bring to the boil and cook till tender.*

*2. Drain away the water and return to a slow heat to dry the potato out.*

*3. Add half of the **butter** and the **nutmeg** and **pepper**. Mash till smooth.*

*4. Add the chopped **herbs**, just at the point of serving.*

*For the Steak and Curly Kale:*

*1. Heat a frying pan with **olive oil**, then add **butter** and fry until golden.*

*2. Add the **steak** and cook to medium rare (or as you prefer).*

38

## Roasted Apples and Pears with Cinnamon Butterscotch Sauce

3. Once cooked remove the **steak** from the pan and allow time to 'relax' (it becomes more tender) in a warm place.

4. Using the same pan add the washed **kale** and sauté till tender, season with **nutmeg** and steam slightly by adding a touch of **apple juice**.

For the Red Onion Jam:

1. Add some **olive oil** to a saucepan and heat with a touch of **garlic**.

2. Next add the **chilli, red onions** and **thyme**. Sauté till soft but without colour.

3. Add the **sugar** and fry for a further five minutes until golden.

4. Add the **red wine (or Port)** and reduce slowly to about half the original measure.

5. Serve the steak on a round of mashed potato topped with sautéed kale. Drizzle the red onion jam over the top and make a simple balsamic dressing around the outside. Top with fresh **watercress**.

*Miserden at the Autumn equinox.*

### Serves 4

2 washed, quartered and cored English apples

2 washed, quartered and cored English pears

2 cloves

1oz (25g) cinnamon

3oz (75g) "Netherend Farm" butter

3oz (75g) Demerara sugar

5fl oz (150ml) "Cotteswold Dairy" whipping cream

Shortbread biscuits

"Winstone's" ice cream

"Hobbs House" fruit bread

1. In a frying pan, melt the **butter** and heat to slightly golden.

2. Add the **apples** and **pears** (skin side down first) with the **cinnamon** and **cloves**.

3. Don't shake the pan, leave the fruits to gain some colour.

4. Next add the **sugar** and start to stir. The sugar needs to coat the fruit and mix with the butter.

5. Once the sugar is all dissolved and starting to caramelise, add the **whipping cream** and stir well. Take care not to mash up the fruit. As the cream boils with the sugar, it will turn to butterscotch sauce.

6. Serve with slices of toasted **fruit bread** and your favourite **ice cream**.

39

Blackstable Woods, Sheepscombe, in January.

Winter and Christmas
Recipes:

Jerusalem Artichoke
Soup

Venison Steak

Celeriac and Double
Gloucester Cheese Bake

Neeps

Christmas Carrots

Rob Rees' Christmas
Pudding

# Winter and Christmas

Cotswold seasons are distinct and different. A long and hard Winter leaves local people longing for Spring but, meanwhile, there are compensations. It can be another time for romantics, with shorter days, country pubs with log fires and quickly taken walks in the low Winter sun before heading back indoors for food, comfort and warmth.

Christmas in the small Cotswold towns and villages is intimate and meaningful. The passing of the shortest day, marking the slow return of the sun, is welcomed. Above all, this is the season for dinner with friends, for gossipy conversation by the fire and the happiness that that brings.

Home cooking in Winter should be all about soups, roasting and baking; warming hearty food with down to earth flavours.

The British pudding is something of a national institution and the British Winter is probably the reason why. Certainly, I find myself giving more time to puddings in the Winter months than at other times of the year. This section includes my family's Christmas Pudding recipe. Even the list of ingredients is full of nostalgia and the magic of Winter.

*Winter trees near Birdlip.*

41

# Jerusalem Artichoke Soup

Serves 6

**1lb (450g) "Duchy Home Farm" Jerusalem artichokes, washed, peeled and sliced**

**1 chopped "Abbey Farm" onion**

**1 chopped rasher of "Duntisbourne Meats" bacon**

**1 sprig of thyme**

**1 tsp nutmeg**

**1pt (575ml) vegetable or chicken stock**

**$\frac{1}{4}$pt (150ml) "Cotteswold Dairy" whipping cream**

**A few chopped chives**

**"Selsley Herb" olive oil**

1. *Sweat the **bacon** and **onion** together in a thick-bottomed pan until tender but not coloured.*

2. *Add the **thyme** and the **artichokes**. Cook for a further minute on a medium heat.*

3. *Cover with the **stock**. Allow to simmer for 12 minutes or till the artichokes are very tender.*

4. *Remove from the heat.*

5. *Place in a liquidizer with the **nutmeg** and purée.*

6. *Once smooth, strain through a sieve.*

7. *Return back to the heat to add the **cream**. Do not boil once the cream is added as it may taint.*

8. *Upon serving, add a few chopped **chives** and a drizzle of **olive oil** for presentation.*

# Venison Steak

Serves 2

**2 x 6oz (175g) "Matthew Wilson's" venison steaks**

**1oz (25g) butter**

**1 chopped clove of garlic and some black pepper**

1. *Heat a pan with the **butter** till it just starts to turn golden.*

2. *Add the chopped **garlic** and cook till soft but not coloured. Add your **venison steaks**. Do not turn the meat in the pan. This is so that you get a golden brown seal to the outside of the meat – that will preserve not only the taste but also the nutritional qualities in the meat.*

3. *Once golden, turn the meat over and repeat on the other side. Cook to your preference, but take care to cook thoroughly. Venison is best served slightly pink in the middle.*

4. *When cooked, give them a twist of **pepper** and serve immediately. Ideal with neeps (recipe page 44) and gravy!*

42

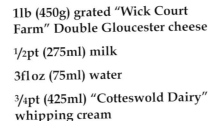

## Celeriac and Double Gloucester Cheese Bake

Serves 6

1 large washed, peeled and thinly sliced "Abbey Farm" celeriac

3 cloves of garlic, chop two and leave the other just peeled

Black pepper

1lb (450g) grated "Wick Court Farm" Double Gloucester cheese

$1/2$pt (275ml) milk

3fl oz (75ml) water

$3/4$pt (425ml) "Cotteswold Dairy" whipping cream

1. Place the sliced **celeriac**, chopped **garlic**, **water** and **milk** into a pan. Bring to the boil then simmer for 2 minutes.

2. Carefully strain away the milk leaving just the celeriac slices.

3. You will need a baking dish at this stage.

4. Wipe the spare **garlic** clove around the entire inside of the dish. This allows the flavour to permeate the baking dish.

5. Layer some of the sliced **celeriac** into the bottom of the dish. Give a twist of **pepper** and cover lightly with grated **cheese**.

6. Repeat this process till the dish is full.

7. Finally top with **cheese** and pour over the **cream**.

8. Cook in a 'Bain Marie' (water bath) in a hot oven until golden brown.

9. Sprinkle with chopped parsley just before serving.

*January blizzard, Brockhampton.*

43

## Neeps

Serves 6

**2 peeled and diced "Duncan Paget" carrots**

**1 peeled and diced "Duchy Home Farm" swede**

**1 tsp of local "Lypiatt House" honey**

**Chopped Winter sage**

**Drizzle of "Selsley Herb" olive oil**

**Pinch of Cajun spice**

**1oz (25g) "Netherend Farm" butter**

*1. Cover the diced **vegetables** with **water** and place on a medium heat.*

*2. Bring to the boil then reduce the heat to allow a gentle simmer. Cook until the vegetables are tender. Use the tip of the knife to test how well cooked the vegetables are.*

*3. Drain off any excess water.*

*4. Return to the heat at a very low temperature. Allow a minute so that all the moisture is removed.*

*5. Mash with a hand masher till smooth. A few lumps won't matter, in fact they give a handmade feel to the neeps.*

*6. Once smooth, add the **butter**, **honey**, and drizzle of **olive oil**.*

*7. Stir into the mix well so that the butter is melted and the honey oozes throughout.*

*8. Remove from the heat until required for serving.*

*9. Simply re-heat with the **Cajun spice** and the **sage** and serve as a base for your Winter meat courses.*

## Christmas Carrots (my variation of Vichy!)

Serves 6

**6 large "Over Farm" carrots, washed, peeled, washed again and sliced**

**1 tsp cracked black pepper**

**1 bay leaf**

**Zest of 1 lime, 1 lemon and 1 orange**

**1/2pt (275ml) natural orange juice**

**1/2pt (275ml) water (or enough to cover) or "Bottle Green" Elderflower Pressé**

**4oz (125g) freshly chopped parsley**

**1 tbsp olive oil**

*Snow drifts, Sevenhampton.*

44

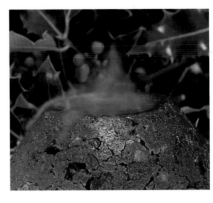

## Rob Rees' Christmas Pudding

*1. Place **all the ingredients** (except the olive oil and parsley) into a saucepan. Ensure that the carrots are just covered with liquid.*

*2. Cover with a lid or greaseproof paper cartouche.*

*3. Place on a gentle simmering heat.*

*4. Cook till all the liquid is reduced and the carrots are tender.*

*5. At point of serving add the **olive oil** and **parsley**.*

The Christmas puddings that we eat nowadays usually come in the shape of the basin in which they are cooked; but when you see pictures of traditional Christmas puddings, they look like large footballs. This is because the pudding mixture was always tied up in a cloth or a bag and then boiled in a large pan, often in the tub that boiled the clothes on washday. As the pudding cooked, it would swell out, until it became round in shape.

Christmas pudding used to be called 'plum pudding' because one of the main ingredients was dried plums or prunes. The name 'plum pudding' continued to be used, even when people started adding raisins, currants, and sultanas instead of prunes.

Puddings, rather like the ones we eat at Christmas, began to appear in the Sixteenth century. Since they were boiled in a bag, they were known as 'bag puddings'. There is a legend about how such puddings came into being. One Christmas Eve an English King found himself deep in a forest with only a little food for his journey. He knocked on the door of a woodman's cottage and asked for food and shelter. The occupant had few provisions, so the King's servant mixed together all the food the woodman could spare with the small amount the King had left. The result was a sticky mixture of chopped suet, flour, eggs, apples, dried plums, ale, sugar and brandy. This mixture was boiled in a cloth and thus a delicious pudding was invented.

45

My recipe for Christmas Pudding is one that has been in the family for many generations. Since a small boy I can recall early November mornings mixing and steaming the traditional dessert with my Nan who really embraced this recipe and made it her own with a very secret ingredient that shall only be passed on to my child when the time is right. My Nan, along with my parents, were my inspiration and motivation to enter the career I chose and it all started over 30 years ago stood on a stool in my Nan's kitchen, licking the Christmas Pudding bowl and having the best fun in the world ever.

This recipe makes approximately five 2 pint pudding basin size puddings – *perfect for gifts!*

½lb (225g) self-raising flour

1lb (450g) breadcrumbs

1lb (450g) suet

1lb (450g) dark brown sugar

1 tsp allspice

12oz (325g) currants

24oz (650g) raisins

6oz (175g) mixed peel

2oz (50g) ground almonds

Grated rind of 2 lemons

¼ grated nutmeg

8 "Cotswold Legbar" eggs

2 tbsps black treacle

Juice of 2 oranges

1 grated "Over Farm" carrot

1 grated cooking apple

3 cans of Guinness, brandy or "Freeminer" Speculation Ale

*1. Mix **all ingredients** in a large bowl and allow to soak overnight.*

*2. Place in a well-greased pudding basin (fill to an inch from the top). Place buttered greaseproof paper, cut to fit the top, wrap in either muslin or tin foil and tie ready for steaming.*

*3. Steam for 10 hours. Re-heat on Christmas Day by steaming for further 5 hours.*

*The key to a dark, moist and rich pudding is in the steaming – the longer you can do it the better it becomes.*

46

# Index

General references in roman type.
**Recipe page numbers in bold type.**

Apples 10, 15
    Roasted Apples and Pears with Cinnamon
    Butterscotch Sauce **39**
Asparagus 12, 23
    Asparagus and Trout Potato Omelette **25**
Artichokes
    Globe 13, 14
    Jerusalem 17
    Jerusalem Artichoke Soup **42**
Bacon
    Gloucester Old Spot 13
Basil 14
Beans 29
    Broad Beans 12, 14 (see also Risotto)
    Green Beans 13
    Runner Beans 14
Beef
    Buying Tips 20
    Fillet Steak with Herb Mash, Curly Kale
    and Red Onion Jam **38**
    Gloucester Breed 14, 20
Beetroot 14, 15, 16
Blackberries 15
Blackcurrants 14
Bread and Butter Pudding **27**
Broccoli 11, 15, 21
Cabbage 12, 15, 16
    Primo Cabbage 12
Caesar Salad 13
Calabrese 11
Carrots 11, 12, 16, 21, 35

Christmas Carrots **44**
Cauliflower 16, 21
Celeriac 16, 35
    Celeriac and Double Gloucester Cheese
    Bake **43**
Celery 16
Chard 15, 17
    Chard, Herb and Celeriac 'Hash' with
    Horseradish Spiced Lamb **31**
Cheese (see also Risotto, Onions, Celeriac)
    Buying 18, 19
    Rolling 20
Chestnuts 15, 17
Chicory 10
Chicken 21
Chives 10
Christmas Pudding 41, **45**, **46**
Chutney 15
Ciabatta Bread and Old Spot Pork Stack **26**
Coriander 14
Cotswold Bread and Butter Pudding **27**
Country Markets 19
Courgettes 13, 14
Cucumber 14
Cuddles 16
Custard 32
Duck 20
Elderberries 15
Farm Shops and Farmers' Markets 9, 18
Fennel 35
Fillet Steak with Herb Mash, Curly Kale
    and Red Onion Jam **38**
Game 10, 16, 20
Garlic (see also wild garlic) 17, 35

Gooseberries 14
Greengages 15
Guinea Fowl 20
Jerusalem Artichoke Soup **42**
Juniper 10
Kale 17, 35
Lamb 11, 20, 23
    Buying Tips 20
    Chard, Herb and Celeriac 'Hash' with
    Horseradish Spiced Lamb **31**
Lavender 29
    Lavender Custard 29, **32**
Leeks 12, 16, 17, 21
Lettuce 10, 12, 13, 14
    Little Gem 13
    Romaine 13
Mange-Tout 13
Marrows 15
Meringue 33
    Marinated Summer Berries with Cotswold
    Meringues **33**
Nasturtium Flowers 14
Neeps **44**
Nettles 30
Old Spot 23 (see also Pork)
    Bacon 13
    Sausages 36 (see also Toad in the Hole)
Organics 18
Onions 35
    Red Onions 15
    Spring Onions 10, 11
    White Onion and Cheddar Cheese Soup **36**
Parsnips 16, 21, 35
Partridge 16

47

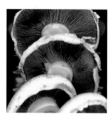

## Contacts

Pears 10, 15, 17
   Roasted Apples and Pears with Cinnamon
   Butterscotch Sauce **39**
Peas 14, 21, 29 (see also Risotto)
Peppers 14
Pheasant 16, 20
Plums 15
Pork
   Buying Tips 20
   Old Spot 16, 20, 23
   Ciabatta Bread and Old Spot Pork Stack **26**
   Toad in the Hole with Gloucester Old Spot
   Sausages **36**, **37**
Potatoes 12, 15, 21
   All Rounders 21
   Floury (King Edward) 21
   Waxy (Cara) 21
Poultry 20
Pumpkin 17
Purple Sprouting 11
Radishes 14
Raspberries 14 (see also Meringues)
Redcurrants 14
Red Onions 15
Red Onion Jam **38**
Rees, Rob
   Training 8
   Christmas Pudding 41, **45**, **46**
   Cookery lessons 9
   Cotswold Chef 8, 9
Rhubarb 11, 23
Risotto
   Risotto of English Peas, Stinging Nettles,
   Broad Beans, Mint and Blue Cheese **30**

Salsify 10
Shallots 10, 19
Shopping Tips 18
Sloes 15
Sorrel 12
Spinach 12, 17, 35
Spring Greens 11
Sprouts 10, 17, 21
Squashes 15
Strawberries 13, 14, 29 (see also Meringues)
   Strawberries in English Tarragon and
   Lavender Custard **32**
Swede 17, 21
Sweetcorn 14
Toad in the Hole with Old Spot
   Sausages **36**, **37**
Tomatoes 14
Trout 11, 15
   Trout and Asparagus Potato Omelette **25**
Turnips 15, 16, 35
Venison 10
   Venison Steak **42**
Valentine's Day 10
Vodka 27
Walnuts 15
Watercress 14
   Watercress and Wild Garlic Soup **24**
White Onion and Cheddar Cheese
   Soup **36**
Whitecurrants 14
Wild Garlic 11, 23
   Wild Garlic and Watercress Soup **24**
Wild Mushrooms 15

You can find more about Rob Rees
and his cooking demonstrations and
the suppliers included in this book
(including additional or alternative
suppliers) at:
**www.thecotswoldchef.com**
or call: 01285 760170

Information on visiting and staying
in the Cotswolds can be found at:
**www.cotswolds.com**

Further copies of this book can be
purchased from Rob Rees or direct
from Darien-Jones Publishing on
01452 812550.

Darien-Jones Publishing
PUBLISHERS OF MAPS & BOOKS

Hillside House · Pitchcombe · Stroud
Gloucestershire GL6 6LN · England
Telephone: (01452) 812550  Fax: (01452) 812690
Email: djp@nicholasjjonesgraphics.co.uk